Stourport
on Severn

Worcester

Upton on Severn

Saxon Lode

Tewkesbury

ND

MALVERN
HILL

Gloucester

Severn
Bridge

Hereford

E

S

N

W

The
Severn

Rivers · of · Britain

The Severn

Thicker than Water

Wilson Stephens

Illustrated by Gabriel White

MULLER, BLOND & WHITE

The Introductory quotation is from *The Welsh Marches* by
A. E. Housman and is reproduced by kind permission of the
Society of Authors, as the literary representative of the Estate
of A. E. Housman and Jonathon Cape Limited, publishers of
A. E. Housman's *Collected Poems*.

First published in Great Britain in 1986 by
Muller, Blond & White Limited
55 Great Ormond Street, London WC1N 3HZ.

Copyright © Wilson Stephens 1986
Illustrations copyright © Gabriel White 1986

British Library Cataloguing in Publication Data

Stephens, Wilson
    The Severn.—(Rivers of Britain)
    1. Severn, River (Wales and England)
    I. Title   II. Series
    914.24   DA670.S29

    ISBN 0–584–11139–8

Printed and bound in Great Britain at The Bath Press, Avon

Springhead

A S much as any river in Britain, Severn has drawn tranquillity round herself, and must indeed be feminine. Free as air through rural Wales — Severn's tomboy phase — she grows in dignity throughout her long pastorale on England's western flank, until her last miles widen amid mists and sandbanks, and become the Severn sea. Past three confident and gracious county towns, first Shrewsbury, then Worcester and Gloucester with their noble cathedrals, Severnside has linked villages along her banks and breathed over them the settled air of established contentment.

It was not always so. The pages of history reveal a darker truth. The element which more than any other dominated Severn's past was blood. No river valley, great or small, in all our islands has been more fought over. Even in summertime on Bredon, those with eyes and ears alert for signs can see the fading scars of old wars that lasted through the centuries after the Romans left and before the Normanised English could establish Pax Britannica in their homeland.

Not only on the face of her countryside but even more clearly in her people's hearts and ways, Severn binds the peaceful present to the violent past.

When Severn down to Buildwas ran,
Coloured with the death of man,
Couched across her brother's grave,
The Saxon got me on the slave.

Thicker than Water

WE who come from Severnside are the offspring of two bloods. In symbol or in deed, some raw act is in all our beginnings: a conquest, a surrender, a victory in reverse; which of them does not matter. We are the heirs of hopes realised and hopes abandoned, of triumph and despair, of those who fought to gain the land we spring from, and of those who died to keep it, leaving something of themselves in us which time has not extinguished from the widest vale in Britain.

Severn herself, from mountain stream to rolling river, has seen the mingling down the years of Saxon and Celt, English and Welsh. After fifteen centuries, that fusion has left its mark on the ground and on the map. It echoes in the lilt of local speech. These are outward signs of something deeper. We, whose ancestral mettle was forged in the coloured counties of the March, still feel a dual affinity in our hearts, a double destiny from those who crudely formed our being.

When killing stops and conquest pauses, those left alive react against the carnage they have survived. It is Nature's reassertion to restore the norm; the response of the life force to the ebb and flow of species. After battle the takers of life are impelled to procreate it, a compensation which long outlasts the initial brutality, and is attested not only by the legends of the past but by the birthrate statistics of our own time. Translated into the reflexes of rough men at a rough moment, the conquerors exert the rights they regard themselves as having won.

So it has been after every war in history, right to our own. So it was when the Romans had gone and the Saxons had come, finding a well ordered land where even the slaves were desirable, and where the people had gone soft after four hundred years of peace; a land given shape, coherence, unity by the great river which the Romans called Sabrina, and the German-speaking infiltrators mispronounced as Severn.

This is the longest river in Britain. Briefly a barrier between the invading Saxons and the resident Romano-Britons, it now unites their successor entities of Wales and England by rising in the Cymric mountains and flowing into an English sea.

In its long travel it encloses what was for centuries the disputed ground of the two most distinctive elements in our modern nation's genealogical mix: the tenacious, practical Saxons who pressed ever westward, and the fervent, imaginative Celts, most of whom, in their fiery pride, at first preferred freedom at the price of poverty in fortified valleys to the shame of cohabitation with people they regarded as barbarians.

No doubt the Saxon land-grabbers seemed a rough lot to those who, under the sophisticated rule of Rome, had known settled lives for as long as now separates us from the Spanish Armada. The Saxons

had obeyed one of humanity's oldest urges, "Go West, young man!" No major human migration in history has ever been to the East.

The urge to seek riches and new homelands follows the sun, and those who answer it are seldom the most polished of individuals. Genghiz Khan and Tamurlane, the Nordic settlements and the opening up of America all took new waves of belligerent humanity westward until oceans or mountains stopped them.

In this case, where the Saxons met the mountains, they had come far enough. They were on fertile ground. The thin soil, the rocky heights, the incoming Atlantic storms and the dark combes ahead had few attractions for them. They had not travelled a thousand miles from the Frisian plains to scratch a living on mountainsides. That wild country could be left to the *wealas*, their name for foreigners.

So they called it Wales, and for the first time Welsh and English existed side by side. Where one began and the other ended varied locally and across the years. Sometimes English communities colonised valleys which led into the mountain fastness, perhaps as military outposts, perhaps for trade. Sometimes the Welsh pushed down from the high ground into the plain, where occasional villages remained true to their ancient names, ancestry, language and customs, though surrounded by immigrant settlers.

For centuries the pressures went first one way, then the other. As time passed, the effect became blurred. Human nature being what it is, and love being more potent than war, marriages took place across the dividing line of race. The acts of rape were replaced by acts of union in every sense. What was happening was not quite the birth of the nation, but certainly the birth of a distinctive part of it.

A new blend emerged in the patchwork of the English people. The faith and hope of the Welsh was upheld by a sense of identity, toughened in the struggle for survival by their genius for song, and by a fiercely poetic language. Intermixed, it irradiated the enduring courage and tenacity of the English.

Whichever was the preponderant blood in their local ancestry, the Anglo-Welsh developed a cohesive communal spirit and a deathless loyalty to their homeland. In the long ago times, when men travelled little, home was not the island on which they lived, but the river valley which comprised all they knew of the world, and the river was their only guide to regions beyond their ken.

So it is that Welsh place names still dot the Saxon shires of Severnside; that my own Anglicised forename derived, four centuries ago, on the bleak hills of Powys, in a village where even now English is a foreign tongue; and that the March (the strip of England which links with Wales) is the last relic in our common speech of Mercia, the Saxon kingdom of which it once formed part. The mixing of the races which brought about such things has produced a strain of Briton distinctive from the rest.

Sabrina blood is a heady blend, and when stirred has produced the stuff of greatness. Those who possess it are inclined to dream their dreams and hold them true. From Severnside came Shakespeare's genius, Elgar's music, Clive's vision of Empire, Abraham Darby's spark which fired the Industrial Revolution. Sabrina folk are people with long traditions; their streak of mysticism is the fallout of a contrasting ancestry, with all the inner vigour that such a combination brings.

Fourteen hundred years have passed since that fusion became established. On first consideration it may seem a long time, but it covers only forty human generations, a short bracket in genetic terms. In any stockbreeding operation, designed to combine the qualities of two breeds, the characteristics of the originals would still be apparent, and so they are in this human accident.

Sabrina folk are in clear contrast to other Britons. Not in them the flat and unadorned attitudes of northerners, the easy-go of Wessex, the Fenlanders' defensiveness, the mercurial cockney mind. Where the cadences of Wales overflow into England, the audible sign of their heritage, the speakers are as much part of the Severn scene as is the long river which gives them their identity.

For me to trace the Severn's course is both a personal testimony and a journey from then to now. Of my thirty-two progenitors, six generations back and three centuries ago, only two came from anywhere but Severnside – a German and a Cornishman, both in my father's line. No non-Severnsider, male or female, intruded since. On Severnside I feel the call of home and an absence of time, as if every sight I see is one which I have always known.

High on the landward slope of Plynlimon Fawr, in bardic lore and modern instinct the most Welsh of mountains, a runnel snakes between ling and sphagnum moss. Climb to the skyline, look westward, and there the Irish Sea lies shining under the sun, embraced in the arms of Cardigan Bay. These few yards, whence the slow brown water seeps, unite three of the four components of the British Isles. Cymru, whose soil it is; England, because this small spring grows to be the Severn; Eire, out of sight but far from out of mind; only Caledonia is missing.

The endless Welsh wind sweeps over the bare mountain. Cotton grass combs it into whispers as it bows and lifts. A curlew bubbles, then is silent for the next hour; an airborne croaking, soon blown away, is the famished raven's cry. A sheep looks at me blank-eyed, as if amazed at finding itself not alone, then bleats and runs off. All that is left is silence and emptiness, the only sign of life the trickle in its winding channel, which will grow until it rears its head in mighty contra-flow as the Severn bore surges upstream above Bristol toward Gloucester.

It is difficult to trace these first wavering steps of the haunting and haunted Severn. They lead from tussock to bog and to tussock again. Often it is wise not to tread too closely. Bog is one thing, quagmire another, but they look much the same.

However, after only two miles a channel can be recognised. Two more miles, and other streamlets have joined the first. The widening, deepening flow has cut itself a little combe. Dwarf oak and stunted alder overhang the tumbled rocks beside it.

The bodily shape of a major river develops in miniature. Pools and stickles and waterfalls, all very small, rehearse for their full scale versions in the miles below. The little waterway speaks now with other tongues.

The stream's own voice is one of these, here big enough to purl and bubble. A dipper bobs on a projecting stone, then flies upstream. A flash of white on black and a voice like an electrical short-circuit. The bold call of a ring ouzel tells me where to look, and there he is, the blackbird of the wilderness, with a white gorget like a High Court usher.

So far, no sign of man. That comes later, at the spot where somebody in years gone by put a stone slab to bridge the stream, thereby admitting its influence on human affairs. In winter, when it and its tributaries came pounding down and brimmed their banks, it had become an obstacle to progress.

The high moors are above me now, the combe cut deep below them by the growing river, which on the map has here attained the rank of "afon". So I must climb out of it to see the wild miles over which my forefathers rode their ponies and watched their sheep across the centuries.

There they developed lean frames, legs and lungs for the hills, and a taste for being alone in the wind, which they have handed down to me. The time came when, like all good livestock, they moved down the valley to richer land below, where grass grows lush and greener, and beasts fatten earlier.

For them, the river was doing a river's work, acting as a great root system carrying the material within its reach, human and otherwise, to places in the sun. That has been Severn's function, to take the tides of life two ways, to splice them, grafting on to us who come of Severn stock the mental and physical heritage of independence, frugal living, hard weather, hard work, and a lean surrounding beauty.

After the forty generations, year after year passes unchanged up in the land of Severn's perpetual youth, as years have always done. Winter skies are dark with storms blown in from the Irish Sea, sometimes heavy with snow; or they are bright with frosty northern weather which no man trusts. In spring the lambs are born on the open hills and

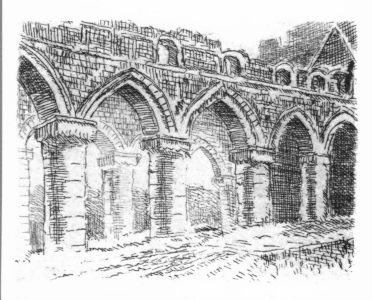

Wales's own daffodils bloom wherever the soil is deep enough, and sheltered.

In summer the hay is made, fleeces are shorn, and the patchwork harvests gathered in, giving the hill farmers a rare experience at this cool height — briefly, they sweat. Autumn comes, and the oaks are yellow; the hills are blinded in the rain. Severn, which has chuckled boyishly through half the year, now roars out the loud tones of a river's manhood.

Near Welshpool the river changes nationality. Reinforced by more water from Wales at the Vyrnwy confluence, it winds across the rich land of north Shropshire passing Melverley and Shrewsbury, flowing into the city under what is still "the

Welsh bridge" and out of it under "the English bridge". Ten river miles downstream, now lost and forgotten by all except historians the Roman cantonment of Uriconium lay on its eastern bank. All memories of its military past are obliterated in Wroxeter, the Nordic village established on its site.

Ten more river miles lead on to Buildwas, where the taint of blood was purged and faded in the years of slaughter. Here, the Wrekin rears up its lonely height, Nature's accidental summit above the surrounding plain. Between it and the uplands to the west, Severn's course is now set southward to the sea.

The Voice of Sabrina

THIS is the Severn which the world knows: the great English river which created the ports of Bristol and Gloucester, and even in the motor age remains a barrier to east-west land travel. From Ironbridge, a technological marvel of the 1770s, all the way down to salt water, bridges average ten miles apart and many more are the extra miles of those who wish to cross.

In places, even now, ferries (no help to heavy traffic) still link villages. All the way the Severn changes. To know it in its various stages is to begin to understand the river's effect on its wide vale.

Until it reaches Shrewsbury its character is pastoral, a part of the farming background through which it passes, with rich crops, and cattle gathering round its cow-drinks at day's end. Below this, its first large town, the weight of its water builds up in winter into savage spates.

The Romans chose shrewdly when they sited Uriconium at the lowest point where the river posed no threat, and where they could rely on crossing by boat whenever they needed. Only a mile or two below, the pastoral scene has been replaced by a gorge. There the winter flow, concentrated between steep banks, rises and falls violently.

In flood the river races down, bearing an overload of wreckage and uprooted trees, and no craft could

live. Bridgnorth and Bewdley, poised steeply over the deep-cut river, have grown up round the next two bridges, but downstream at Stourport the banks open up and Severn, striding along in full grandeur, is re-united with the surrounding fields.

The bigger it grows, the fewer and farther between are the bridges. From Stourport to Worcester, Worcester to Tewkesbury, and Tewkesbury to Gloucester there is only one bridge in each section. Downstream of Gloucester only the Severn suspension bridge itself, carrying the motorway to Wales, fights for survival against the winds which funnel up the wide estuary and rock it as they pass.

Such is the Severn in synopsis; not only a divider but a unifier too. At its widest its vale stretches from Warwick far into Wales, at its longest from the Cheshire border to the Bristol Channel. This far-flung and varied area is as large as the West Country, Yorkshire, East Anglia, the Scottish Borders, or any other of the distinctive regions of the British Isles. It is just as self-contained.

The recognition sign which defines it is heard not seen, the tell-tale intonation of Wales superimposed on English words. At full purity in the villages of the March, still present though distorted in the dialect of Birmingham and the Black Country, it is the birthmark of the folk whose ancestral mix was decided when the Romans withdrew, leaving two bloods to spill, then to mingle, and their progeny to spread outward to the Severn vale's distant rims.

Speech, the outward audible sign of the inner fact of heritage, has spread along the lie of the land. The psychic presence of Wales extends much farther eastward into England than the map indicates, and simple observation makes this evident. It has survived the tides of history because realities made it do so. The greatest of these has been the countryside of southern Shropshire.

The infiltrations into Severnside during the sixth and seventh centuries were of German-speakers motivated by the everlasting German search for living space, for ever pressing on. Our own nation, being then German-derived, acted likewise centuries later; the immediate consequences were the British Empire, the secondaries the self-governing Dominions and the Englishness of the United States. The pioneers among those who seek living space naturally stake prior claim to the best, and fight for it if necessary.

So the early waves of Severnside immigrants came to the river, and crossed it. Using it as a guide line, they took over first the rolling countryside of north Shropshire, and the red-soiled vales of trans-Sabrina Gloucestershire and Herefordshire. Time confirmed their judgment. Their descendants made north Shropshire into prime cornland, Gloucestershire and Herefordshire world-renowned for their stock farming.

These two districts are separated by thirty miles of uplands, as defiant of the plough as they have been resistant to the will of man expressed in other ways. It has been well said that the rocks remain. Here, still, they present to us a sight not very different from that which confronted those in-

comers who, in their search for homelands, crossed the Severn within ten miles upstream or down of Bridgnorth.

Anywhere, in that sector, hills bar the way westward, hills which are intersected by steep little dales (on the Welsh side of the March they would be cwms) and overlook the river flowing five miles off. From the very first summit the view ahead is no longer that of a land of milk and honey, nor is it the good rich earth which qualified as England; it is the same high and beautiful wildness which is Wales, into which the retreating Britons took their cherished freedom, but here has been left behind in an English county by the human tide.

One beyond another, coloured by sunshine and cloud shadow, ridge behind ridge stretches away. Their names define the Sabrina heartland — the Clee, Wenlock Edge, the Long Mynd, the Stiperstones, Long Mountain, Clun Forest — names that bespeak an everlasting wind. Beyond them all is Wales, from this viewpoint more than ever a land of strangers.

High up here, across half a county, autumn and winter are tawny with bracken, summer briefly purple when the ling is blooming. England's southernmost grouse burst from it with rattling wings. Over it the ceaseless cries of sheep are the majority voice of the Sabrina country.

These are lonely heights, where the primeval has not faded. Small brooks, still in a state of nature, curl between the hillsides, brooks which are almost extinct on the farmed land below, where land drains have replaced them. In the dales which separate the ridges flow larger streams whose names echo the Celtic past — Ledwyche, Corve, Onny, and Clun.

They were so-called before the invaders came; likewise some of the villages and hill tops. Llwyn, Bryn, and Caer Caredoc are among those holding fast after centuries to their pre-Roman identity, long since islanded among Englishness where the Saxons good-naturedly allowed the old speech and customs to continue undisturbed. Small wonder that the tincture of Celtic blood stirs in their people's hearts.

Celtic Fire, Solid Saxon

TO be Celtic is to be imaginative, to see pictures in the mind, stirred by communal memories long handed down, and to trust insight as readily as reason. The feelings of all Celts run deep, and are fiercely underlined. They are faithful to their beliefs, and belief to a Celt is a burning of the soul.

Where the Saxon accepts, the Celt challenges; where the Saxon adapts the Celt holds fast. So when the Saxons proved no weaklings when it came to holding fast for themselves, the Celts remembered and reacted.

To stand on Brown Clee Hill, just short of the eighteen-hundred foot contour, and to etch the detail of the surrounding scene with my own share of Celtic imagination, gives me a vision of Severnside in the making. Its present scenes recreate the past before the eyes of the modern beholder. The four-way view is full of contrasts.

Northward the land falls away to the corn country, with Shrewsbury in its centre. Eastward lies Worcestershire with its bottomless soil, the orchard of England, its underrated beauties embellished in spring by miles of plum and apple blossom cushioning the quiet villages. To the south is the red soil of Herefordshire and lowland Gloucestershire.

Westward, across Corvedale, the sun lights up the tawny Clun hills and, beyond them, blue with distance, the Cymric mountains, a sight to lift the heart. Between the tawny and the blue, with the Saxon's sure eye for the distinction between one countryside and the next, King Offa of Mercia built his dyke in the ninth century to separate the English on its east from the Welsh on its west.

This great wall and ditch, still evocative of toil and sweat after a thousand years' disuse, runs from west of Chester to Chepstow, a man-made parallel to the Severn itself as a barrier between the races, but re-establishing the frontier thirty-five miles westward. Its digging and fortifying must have been an immense task for the still sparse immigrant population, preoccupied with their pioneer farming and lacking all resources except hand tools and gumption.

What it achieved militarily cannot have been much. But it did establish that a Welshman east of it, or an Englishman west, was conspicuously trespassing.

Evidently there was no lack of trespass. What happened on one side was repeated on the other. To balance the Welsh village names left behind in England, English names became scattered farther and farther up the valleys into Wales.

Language can move only where its speakers carry it. The great dyke, like the river, changed from obstacle into link. For centuries peace between the two races existed only by being enforced, but that in itself meant contact, and the human ties between those who met there, on whatever errand, could not be prevented. The rivalry and the unity both remain.

The March, and Magic

WHATEVER the English can do, the Welsh can do better; and vice versa. This evident truth remains the thinking on the March. The determination to excel the other side has invigorated both for a thousand years. Raids from the mountain men of Wales, forays in revenge by Englishmen ever surer of their ground, wars and counter-wars between their rulers, criss-crossed for centuries the vale that both sides knew as home. Although the forays are reduced to rugby football now, the imprint of bygone conflict is clear on the land.

That strange term, the March, suggests the tramp of armies that was so often heard in the land to which it applies. But it did not derive as such. At first it expressed merely the limit, the margin to the area taken over by the German-speaking newcomers, leaving Mercia as the name of the Anglo–Saxon kingdom beyond the eastern and southern regions which were settled first. The Mercians were the frontiersmen among the emergent English, a role which long outlasted Mercia itself.

So I look down from this high hill on Severnside. What I see and what I feel involve the permanent and the transient, the ancient and the new. Together they compose something distinct and different, materially and spiritually separate from the rest of Britain.

The land of Sabrina lies there as a reality revealed to us natives not only by our inherited Celtic instincts, but by our share of the magnetism which holds Severnsiders of either blood or both to their native soil. This is where the air, the soil, and the plants combine to produce the feel and the smell of the land which those ancestors knew, whose heritage I embody. I have only to come back to know that I belong here; only to breathe to know that I am home.

The westerly wind breathes its message back. On four days out of five it is a permanent feature of Sabrina, pouring into the great vale from Wales, from Ireland and mid-ocean, a cool and lively wind which sets grass and leaves and branches moving, and in high places lifts the buzzards and the crows.

Nearly everywhere I look, here on the Shropshire side, the nearer view is touched with gold, symbolic of the wilderness that men have tamed. This might be different east of the river, where the gentler countryside allows land to be more highly farmed, but here the hills, the rocky outcrops and the loops of streams leave rough patches that go back to Nature, which means broom and furze.

Yellow blossom, flowering throughout the year, its fragrance lacing air that is so seldom still, colours the counties of the March. It gives its names to towns, villages and hamlets where it grew richly at their inception. Enough Broomes, Bromfields and Bromhams, as well as Broomy-this and Broomy-that are scattered across the March, in addition to prosperous Bromyard and Bromsgrove, to demonstrate how the countryside looked as its forests were felled and each wave of settlers opened up more fields for farming.

In new clearings broom appeared where trees had been. Furze took over on uncultivateable hills. It was no wonder that Henry the Second, that quick-witted energetic king, prompt to see everything that brightened life, and much preoccupied with the Welshmen beyond his border, took the pre-dominant colour of the March as his emblem. He chose, characteristically, something small and simple, a sprig of broom, *planta genista* in the monks' Latin. Hence his dynasty was called Plantagenet.

In the ever-blowing wind, up and down that ex-hilarating countryside, he and the kings before and after him were for ever on the watch, for ever on the move, and often in battle or skirmish. The Welsh border was for England in medieval centuries what the North-West Frontier of India became for the years of the British raj.

The trouble-makers inhabited the hills and, on their own ground, were undefeated. Even when Edward the First followed the sensible doctrine "if you cannot beat them, join them" by creating the Principality and Prince of Wales, the Welsh insur-gence was only partly defused. Six hundred years later Welshmen were still expressing their ancient impulses by burning the holiday cottages of English folk, and calling it an act of piety.

Earlier kings had found Offa's Dyke leaking Welshmen like a sieve. They wrote it off as a de-fensive measure and the Marcher lords came into being. King after King, first Saxon then Norman, set up his own exponents of delegated protection.

The system was to grant land in the trouble zone to noblemen tough enough to stand no nonsense in their neighbourhoods. They were then left to get on with the job of defending their interests, which were also English interests broadly speaking, few questions being asked about how they did it. From north to south down the March the Welsh faced a line of formidable feudal families whose first duty was to keep them out. Their names inspired awe in friend and foe — Constantine, Bagot, Mortimer (most dreaded name of all for more reasons than its association with death), d'Abitot, Lacy and Clifford.

Almost literally, their footprints remain on the March. Place names repeatedly keep them alive. Men robust enough to keep the Welsh at bay did not always maintain diplomatic relations with each other.

Modern maps are graphic synopses of March history, for periodically one family would annexe a village claimed by another, labelling it to denote who was in possession. Stanton Lacy, Hope Bagot, Cleobury Mortimer, are all grouped around the age-old trouble spot of Ludlow. There are many more.

Marcher lords were much on the move — supporting each other, intimidating each other, beating each other up as well as blocking off the Welsh, and electing themselves owners of any property they fancied. Not always was it anything so prosaic as a village.

One of the first of them, Earl Sweyn, an appointee of King Canute, caused no small scandal by including in his acquisitions the good-looking Abbess of Leominster. Recording the affair, the Anglo–Saxon Chronicle noted laconically that he "had her as long as he list" then returned her to the convent, perhaps a more broad-minded abbess.

Another place name acts as a marker for military history. Hereford now denotes to most people the cathedral city which is capital of the county of that name. But there are many other Herefords. Some, recorded only on large-scale maps, are reduced to field-names now. Others might as well be spelled with a small 'h'.

Always there is a stream nearby, for the word means no more than a crossing place (ford) for the heer (army). That ancient German word survives, largely forgotten, in our language from the days when the former mercenary soldiers of Rome moved in to colonise the territories in which they had served and which had been left unguarded by their departed former employers.

Hill-top tracks are still called 'herapaths' — the routes along which the armies could make forced marches to outflank their enemies. We little realize how often we speak forgotten history; or how far blood, so much thicker than water, unites both sides in warfare with tongue the conclusive evidence.

Peaceful now, prospering around its contented villages, Severnside is thus the most blood-soaked part of Britain. Lawless as the Scottish border was, its population, small and scattered, made it the scene of violent crime rather than the organised campaigning which for hundreds of years made the March a constant battlefield.

As the lines of engagement swung from east to west and back again, the breadth of the March itself increased. From being a mere line, as King Offa hoped to keep it, it grew to be a disputed strip, miles wide, bordered by north–south lines through Shrewsbury and Leominster on the east, Corwen and Newtown on the west. The most visible of all evidence confirms that fact today.

A Duel of Castles

EAST of Severn, castles are rarities; west of the river they are commonplace. Most of them are levelled now. Only a few crudely masoned stones, or a misshapen hummock breaking the symmetry of a skyline tell where they stood. But some remain. They stand as monuments to the hundreds of bloodstained years, and the thousands of bloodstained men, who lie behind us in the ancestries of Severnside.

Castles were the power bases of the Middle Ages, standing like land-anchored battleships, defiant and impregnable while wars raged round them, their garrisons the trump cards which could turn a battle when the drawbridges were lowered and fresh, well-armed, disciplined men sallied forth to fight. While a castle remained unconquered, the enemy had not won, even though he controlled the surrounding territory.

In days before long-range artillery, the beseiging of a castle was a fearsome business. It was a choice between hand-to-hand fighting, with the odds favouring the defenders, or starving them out, with the attendant risk of the beseigers being attacked from the rear by an ally or relieving force of their foes. Armies in those days had to keep moving to be safe. To be stationary, unless inside a castle, invited disaster.

So a castle was a prime necessity for any man of war. It had to be something more than merely a fortified house, needing living space for troops and their horses, food enough to stand a seige, supplies of arms and armour. But castle-dwellers did more than merely fight.

Castles were the equivalent in their time of our modern corridors of power. In them the local magnates also plotted and wooed. History's outlines were decided in their dark towers; the blanks were filled in violently outside.

Visiting the castles of the March today, only an insensitive person could be immune to the emanations of their past. In the rooms and passages enclosed in their cold stones men and women of every human quality and failing lived dangerously and died strangely, as Time laid an iron hand on kings.

The bloodstains which splashed the walls have been washed out by centuries of English weather. The arras which lined them has faded and perished. The oaths, the shouting, the death rattles, the cries of tortured prisoners have long since died away. The hammer blows of beseiging sappers, the thud of battering rams, the ricochet of crossbow bolts, the hiss of flaming arrows, the clash of axe and sword had grown faint in memory even before old age claimed the survivors.

Only the jackdaws' voices now raise a parody of soldiers' ribaldry high on the wind-blown battlements, where defiant banners waved. What made the castles live is dead. But what made us live was partly formed in them. By responding as we do, we give the castles their life for as long as we stand before them or walk their ramparts, knowing what we know.

Here were deployed the machinations of desperate and crafty men, of heroes and villains, of designing women and of gentle ones. Humble men did their duty and died doing it. Among the great men, it was one of the Mortimers who planned, unashamedly, to wade through slaughter to a throne, only to perish in the attempt.

Valour, treachery, chivalry, brutishness, cowardice and cruelty were all paraded, seen for what they were and for the most part accepted as the way of the world. Whether as instruments of fate or expressions of the human condition, the castles had it all. Moreover, unlike most lesser structures, some of them still stand.

As men differ, so do the castles of the March, now that their violent past is ended. They are essentially an English institution, built on English soil, impregnated with English history. The Welsh had less need of them, trusting their labarynthine mountains to provide strong-points as well as refuges.

In its day — manned, armed and charged with defiance — an English castle was formidable to see. Drawbridge raised, portcullis dropped, barbican barricaded, the glint of helmets at every battlement and, dominating all else, the great warhead jutting round its central tower, the message was simple: "Come if you dare!" Now, like old soldiers, they have mellowed with advancing years. Hindsight helps to interpret their expressions, but not much of it is needed.

Powys, whose princes sided first with one side then the other, sometimes with both simultaneously, keeping their lives, their titles and their possessions intact across half a millenium, has so bland a look that one hardly needs telling that it was a habitual survivor. Berkeley now is wreathed in peace, its "shrieks of an agonising king" forgotten. Stokesay, now radiant as a bride, is an abode of gentleness, not of force.

Only scattered stones remain of Richard's Castle, named after its builder. Richard Fitzscrob, one of

the Normans who arrived before William the Conqueror, was invited over by Edward the Confessor when even that prayerful monarch could see the need for more and better Marcher lords.

Older still was Bishop's Castle, given away in the reign of Offa himself by Egwin Shakehead as a thanks-offering to the Bishop of Hereford. In that See he had been cured of palsy, thus losing his malady although retaining his surname. The huge bulk of Clun is deadpan.

Of the March castles still upstanding, Ludlow stays most true to form. Its hewn stones whitened now by age, yet stout-walled and immensely strong, it still personifies some great warrior, grey and old, invincible and proud, gazing slit-eyed toward Wales. To test the truth of it, stand to the eastward in the evening.

As the sun goes down in splendid fear beyond the billowing Kerry hills, that scarred but unconquered tower soars arrogant against the light. Then feel the centuries roll away, and know that all around is a land that had no peace for seven hundred years.

Peace at the Last

THE peace it has now is guarded jealously. Severnside has seen humanity expend its savagery. Its people long ago learned gentler values. West of the river, life's pace eases. Old ways seem best, and the line is blurred between past and present. Attitudes lost and outdated elsewhere are normal custom here. The Saxon lust for home soil combines with the mystic Celtic element in holding fast to long accepted hopes and fears, beliefs and legends.

Here the broom is more than just a gallant sight, its golden glory dancing to the wind. It has connotations, long worn away elsewhere, which still bring secret smiles to many a girl's face as she thinks her inner thoughts, even though she may be listening to a transistor radio at the time, in some such village as those which a poet called the quietest places under the sun.

"When the pods go pop on the broom, green broom" the message is that time is ripening. The king who used a sprig of it to identify himself was an incomer and did not know that before his day, as ever afterwards even down to ours, to give a sprig of broom has been perquisite of ladies, and when given means only one thing.

The fidelity of Severnsiders to things which are bygone elsewhere seems natural in a countryside so conscious of its background. Some towns have reeves instead of mayors, court leets as well as councils.

Since the Second World War a lord of the manor of Ratlinghope for a time would have no grouse shot on the Long Mynd. Though well aware of the development of firearms, indeed none better, he preferred another way. His friends rode out on horseback with him, as I have done. Some had falcons on fist. Dog men padded after the horses, with setters on leash.

Behind the dog men trotted the cadger, holders of which ancient office used to expect something for their efforts and gained an unflattering reputation for persistence in demanding it. He carried the wooden frame on which the falcons-in-waiting perched, waiting their call to action. Some slight infusion of the twentieth century was provided by a Land Rover which came last of all, bearing the refreshments.

The setters ranged the heather-clad Mynd to locate the grouse at a distance. When they pointed, their tails flag-high in signal, a falcon was cast-off. She gained height, flying in circles, waiting-on above the dogs statue-still below. When the falcon was settled into flight a dog was ordered to flush the grouse.

Then the falcon would stoop out of the sky in her unerring dive, more deadly than a shot, which killed instantly. The grouse went spinning broken-backed into the heather, the falcon soared in triumph as was the manner of ancient times, indeed of Nature.

Nobody, whether participant or spectator, saw eccentricity, or any other aspect of play-acting in this. If grouse were to be taken at all, this was the way to do it, in local opinion. Though our garb was less splendid, had any reincarnated Tudor ghosts passed our way they would have recognised exactly what we were doing. Such is the way of life which centres on the Severn. Like the river itself, it continues, and time is not exhaustive.

A Modest Pride

IT is not the Severnside manner to publicise the
virtue of Severnside things. If it were, there would
be a world demand for perry. As it is, the world is
well aware that cider is produced in Devon and
Somerset, indeed has become a folk symbol there.
The world is fortunately less aware of the cider
which is produced in Gloucestershire, for which the
heads of non-Severnsiders are unlikely to be strong
enough, and scarcely aware at all of perry.

This princely Herefordshire drink, made from
pears, is too good to be wasted on a global market. Its
sparkling version makes champagne a second choice
to those for whom tasting is believing — a light and
exhilarating, but full and fruity refreshment which
has no superior in making glad the heart of man. At a
bowling green beside the river, where the match-
book has been kept since the reign of the first Queen
Elizabeth (and where it is to be hoped that they did
not play bowls in the ruffianly manner tolerated by
Sir Francis Drake), no man would be bold enough to
play an end unless his nerves had first been steadied
by a glass or two of this, the gambler's friend.

No clearer communal demarcations exist than
tastes in food and drink. Into every English river,
elvers swim in spring. They are infant eels, hatched
in the weed-crammed Sargasso Sea off Florida,
whence they drift on the Gulf Stream across the

Atlantic towards Europe, seeking freshwater in which to grow to maturity. But in Britain, only on Severnside are elvers a delicacy.

In spring, their arrival season, watch is kept on the river from Tewkesbury downstream to Gloucester. Where the current runs close to the banks, hand-held nets scoop elvers out in thousands, so that a day's catch can be measured in hundredweights. Then every Severnside inn for miles advertises elver feasts. Elver pie goes well with ale.

How came the demand for elvers to the Sabrina country, but not to other English valleys? Full-grown eels are on menus anywhere, the most nourishing of all fish. But elvers only here. The taste for them could have come with the Saxon settlers, fifteen-hundred years ago.

While the Sabrina people incorporated their mixed blood, and found their identity separate from other Britons, they may well have kept on eating elvers in springtime as one small strand in that identity. Whence? At Sharpness, below Gloucester, Dutch fish-boats moor in springtime. They arrive empty, sailing up the Severn to buy elvers in bulk and take them back to Holland. There folk have a taste for elvers. And it was from Frisia, now Holland, that some of the Saxons came.

Old ways of life die hard, folk say. Some of them do not die at all. And if the small and unimportant among them can survive, greater characteristics are likely to be as indestructible; such as, for instance, the heritage of Saxon and of Celt, that incandescent mixture throughout Severnside.

Illustrations

BUTTERCUP'S DIARY ANI

Introduction

'Buttercup' is an elderly wooden dinghy, a West Wight scow built in 1951. The first part of this book is made up of extracts from her diary, patiently transcribed by her current caretaker, Claudia Myatt. Buttercup is ever so slightly vain and believes her skipper to be well intentioned but incompetent.

Claudia describes herself as an amateur sailor (Buttercup would agree) who draws boats for a living, and occasionally writes about them too.

Once Buttercup has had her say, Claudia finally gets a word in to take up the story of her sailing days on the East Coast, the inspiration for many of her popular cartoons.

Author's note

You won't learn anything about sailing by reading this book, but hopefully it will add to your enjoyment of messing about in boats.

Contents

BUTTERCUP'S BIRTHDAY

Although built on the Isle of Wight, Buttercup spent much of her life on the East Coast, becoming part of the fleet of Burnham scows on the River Crouch in Essex. For her fiftieth birthday, her skipper had the bright idea of taking her back to Yarmouth to sail with the other West Wight scows and join in the fun of the Yarmouth Old Gaffers Festival. Well, it seemed like a good idea at the time.......

Friday 1st June 2001

It's my birthday. Well, not today exactly, but sometime this year. Fifty years ago, in a Cowes boatyard, my humble frames were planked up and there I was, small but perfectly formed, West Wight Scow no. 92. My skipper, bless her little thermal socks, decided to celebrate by taking me back to the Isle of Wight to sail with the rest of the scow fleet in Yarmouth. There's a classic yacht rally on, so that was all the excuse she needed. What excitement! I've been cooped up on the East Coast for so long I can't remember what it's like to sail in the wide open spaces of the Solent.

Buttercup showing an impressive speed to windward

I won't dwell on the discomfort of hurtling down the M3 at speeds that would have made my shipwrights boggle, but the ferry ride over the Solent gave me the chance to rest my aching frames and experience the bizarre sensation of being a boat on a boat. Finally, we arrived and rigged up, then with a sigh of relief I slid off my trailer and into Yarmouth harbour. Skipper jumped in and hoisted sail straightaway, leaving her family to park the car, stow the trailer and hang around on the quayside while she sailed around amongst the fleet of classics, showing me off to perfection. That's what I like, a skipper with priorities.

The harbour was packed with lovely classics dressed overall; they were all a lot bigger than me, but I always feel at home amongst quality.... after all, size isn't everything. We stopped for a gossip with 'Nancy Blackett', Arthur Ransome's favourite boat and a fellow east coaster (so nice to have friends with literary connections, don't you think?) but then I couldn't resist a quick peep outside the harbour walls.

It was late afternoon with a light westerly wind and the Solent beckoned; it made my planks tingle. Memories stirred and after being cooped up on the muddy old Crouch for years this was heady stuff! Freedom at last! We headed out to sea, but all too soon she remembered her family and turned back. How very annoying, I was just getting into my stride.

We turned back and sailed through the harbour. Skipper had arranged for me to have a mooring amongst the local scows at the Yarmouth Sailing Club, but there was a lifting road bridge between the harbour and the moorings, which are on the river. She stopped to consult the harbourmaster who told her that at this state of tide we'd get through fine without a bridge lift. It didn't look like it to me, but she always believes a man in uniform so we sailed on towards the bridge. This bridge looked low. Very low, and it was full of early evening sightseers all watching the pretty little sailing boat heading towards it. Skipper started to look panicky as the truth began to dawn, but there was no turning back with a tide under us. Crash! My gaff smacked the bridge full on and jammed in the ironwork. Tugging frantically on the halliard she tried to untangle me, much to the amusement of the crowd on the bridge. So embarrassing! I do hope none of the other scows saw this happen. My poor varnish!

"OUCH!"

Eventually she got me free and we drifted through sideways with my skipper buried under spars and sail, struggling to get control of the tiller. I had to find a mooring for her whilst she tried to regain her composure. Obviously the harbourmaster meant that the bridge had clearance for a scow mast but not hoisted sail which is, of course, several feet higher. How stupid can you get? 'Well, how was I to know?' She muttered in a sulk as she stowed my sails for the night and tried to thumb a lift ashore.

Her family was waiting by the sailing club. 'Everything alright?' they asked. 'Oh, fine, no problem!' I heard her say. I'll give her 'no problem' with my gaff smarting painfully and half its varnish scratched with nasty grey paint!

Saturday 2nd June 2001

The next day all was forgiven. I got chatting to the local boats; there were a few wooden ones but most of them were fibreglass youngsters who gave my gleaming varnish envious glances. I must say they all made me feel very welcome; it's so nice to get back to one's roots. Skipper had entered me for a race in the afternoon, which set her panicking because the weather was a bit unsettled. Well, you know what she's like - anything above a force two has her cowering in the yacht club bar drinking gin and saying things like 'well, she's a very old boat and a bit delicate; I'd love to go out, of course, but for her sake I'd better not risk it.... ' which is craven cowardice.

This time, of course, she didn't want to lose face with the locals, who all look very experienced and game for anything. So only I could hear her knees knocking as we hoisted sail and followed the others out of the harbour.

Buttercup's race strategy – make sure you have someone to follow to show you the way.....

Luckily the wind was light to start; she didn't know where the course was, as usual, but that wasn't a problem as there were plenty of boats to follow. In fact, the wind died completely after the start leaving us drifting on the tide, completely confused about which buoy we were aiming for even supposing we had the remotest chance of rounding it. All this took place outside the Royal Solent Yacht Club, which is where the first scows were sailed over 60 years ago. Sailing history laid out before me and all I could do was drift backwards!

Then came wind, but very soon there was too much of it and from the north so we felt rather exposed. The other scows gave a yell of delight and romped off ahead. I'd have been happy to follow - after all, I was designed for these waters! Not a chance - Madam skipper lost it completely and clutched my tiller with white knuckles, completely terrified. She turned and headed for the harbour entrance, shouting across to the others (failing to sound suitably casual because her teeth were chattering with fright) that she was retiring from the race.

Now this did get rather tricky as we were dead downwind, going too fast in a lumpy sea towards a harbour entrance which was almost blocked by a fleet of large motor yachts going round in circles. They were doing this because the 'Harbour full' sign was up and the harbourmaster in his launch was gesturing politely at them all to go away, which under the circumstances they were rather reluctant to do. On board the motor yachts you could hear the tinkling of broken glass and falling ice buckets as white faced wives tried to stop the potted petunia from joining the mess of nibbles and aperitifs on the cabin floor.

Finally my skipper did the only sensible thing since starting the race, which was to turn into wind and drop the sail. This in itself was quite tricky in a confused sea and for a while it looked as though I was about to come to an undignified end in pieces on the harbour wall. Amazingly, she finally got the sail down, the oars out and managed to row us clear.

It was a relief to get inside the harbour and tie up at the pontoon where her husband and son were waiting. 'How did you get on?' they asked. 'Oh, fine, fine, no problem!' she said brightly. 'Just decided not to finish the race, that's all!'

So much for fame and glory and the old school tie..... if they all think Burnham scows are wimps, it certainly won't be my fault!

LANDLOCKED!

Friday 7th June 2002

I view being heaved out of the water and onto my trailer with mixed feelings; it's uncomfortable and usually means an unpleasant, seemingly endless trip by road, but it's also exciting as it means new places to sail. Some summers I spend all season on my mooring and never go out of the Crouch, but today we were off to somewhere new. It turned out to be Rutland Water—not the sea at all! Non tidal? Fresh water? No mud!! This was going to be interesting. We stopped the car on a lovely big slipway and I was desperate for my skipper to get these nasty tight straps off, stop gossiping with that Drascombe lugger owner and get me rigged!

Forgotten anything?

9

Finally we were ready (she forgot the burgee first time, of course) and into the water… that was *so* much better. We rowed over to a pontoon and I began to have misgivings; there may have been no mud here but the pontoon was simply *covered* in duck poo! I just had to hope she checked her shoes before stepping on board.

We appeared to be at some kind of Swallows and Amazons weekend. Skipper's son was wearing a striped hat and doing things with pirate flags while skipper chatted to a crowd of enthusiastic eccentrics trying to brew up cups of tea on wobbly camping stoves under boom tents. Anyone who thinks that sailing is a glamorous sport involving gleaming yachts, muscled Johnny Depp look-alikes and bikini babes should take a look at my typical weekend. Don't get me wrong, we do have a good time, but it's all thermal undies, soggy sandwiches and beer bottle tops in the bilges with my lot.

Ah…. the glamour of yachting……

The Drascombe, a Devon yawl, a Mirror and various other small boats of dubious parentage have assembled. None of them have quite my pedigree, of course.

10

Saturday 8th June 2002

Light winds and a lovely sunny day - I was itching to get out and explore! Skipper and others seemed to spend ages talking but finally we got under way. There was no racing; our game today was to sail wherever we liked and fill in as much of a blank chart of the lake as possible. This was great - wide open spaces so we could sail to the wind, and no tides to worry about. This lake is huge! I set my sights on the far horizon but annoyingly the wind fell away and all too soon skipper decided it was time to turn back and meet the others for lunch. Bloody picnics. I get left on a duck infested pontoon just so she can spend hours eating, drinking and nattering. Don't these humans realise just how much time they spend partying and how little time they spend actually sailing??

The wind was even lighter in the afternoon but we had a lovely drift round the corner up the other arm of the lake, pausing to swap cameras with another boat—what a good idea. I think the pretty wooded banks will have set my yellow foredeck off a treat.

Which is my best tack, I wonder?

We were back to the pontoon all too soon and off they went for the night. I didn't sleep a wink of course, had to spend the entire night glowering at the ducks to make sure they didn't even *think* about messing on my varnish.

Sunday 9ᵗʰ June 2002

It was pouring with rain and blowing hard today. The skippers spent most of the morning huddled ashore playing games with semaphore signals. Every so often someone would say hopefully 'It seems to be clearing up a bit!' but it was lunchtime before the rain stopped. It was still blowing half a gale (well alright, a blustery force 4 but I'm only little and the gusts were mean).

We had a brief but hectic time on the water playing some unfathomable game with the other boats which involved exchanging plastic bottles with messages in them. The skipper and crew seemed to know what they were doing, but it kept me on my toes, I can tell you. I had my work cut out trying to avoid getting my varnish chipped as we came alongside the other boats, and while skipper and son were faffing around with the bottles I was the one who had to make sure we didn't gybe. Quite a lively morning.

After lunch it was back on the trailer (ouch, those straps!) and off home. So much water in the world, so little time!

THAT'S SHOWBIZ!

Friday 5th July 2002

My favourite day of the week - sailing in the morning and then sailing in the afternoon. In theory at least - according to the skipper it's either too windy, in which case we don't go, or not windy enough, in which case we don't go. It's a wonder we ever go sailing at all!

Anyway, this Friday was a bit different. For a start the weather was perfect, which makes a change. In the morning we met up with some of the other scows for a potter down the river, then in the afternoon she took me off to the Burnham Sailing Club as usual where she helps out with the junior session.

Now, I'm all for encouraging youngsters to get afloat, but you would not believe the things I have to put up with sometimes— like reaching up and down the river with a cargo of six year olds who ask stupid questions like 'Can't it go any faster?' or 'Will we capsize?' or, just at the furthest point from the pontoon, 'Can we go in now, I need the toilet!'

But I'm very patient, and they have to learn. They wiggle my tiller until my pintles ache and leave unspeakably sticky sweet wrappers in my bilges, but I try to show my breeding and good manners and not tip the little darlings into the water.

On this particular day there seemed to be more people than usual fussing about on the pontoon, then I noticed a television cameraman in the launch following us as we sailed up and down. Apparently there was a television documentary about sailing being made and they wanted to film children learning to sail. The launch followed the Optimist fleet for a while then turned their attention to my payload of under 8's. Well! I wish she'd given my varnish a polish. I do hope the camera was filming my best side; I didn't really want my split plank to starboard to be recorded for posterity - cameras can be so unflattering.

I made sure I was sailing my best, of course, glad that it was early in the year and I was not held back by weed (being broad in the beam I do have a problem with my bottom occasionally). My new yellow jib looked very fetching, too; what my skipper lacks in sailing finesse she makes up for in generosity, I'm pleased to say.

When we got back to the pontoon, the camera team decided they wanted to take me out and shoot some film. At last my talents are being recognised - today, Discovery Channel, tomorrow, Hollywood! Ooh, the excitement.....

They wanted to do some commentary first so the skipper gave them some background. She was obviously miffed that they wanted to film me and not her, because when the presenter said '.... and this is Buttercup, a West Wight scow owned by Claudia, 51 years old....' my skipper yelled 'It's the boat that's 51 years old, not me!' 'Cut!' groaned the director.

Finally, the commentary was done but it took time to get the cameraman wedged into place forward of the thwart, with all his gear and fluffy microphone thingy. I hoped he could manage to film while sitting in a puddle with his knees round his ears (and without doing himself a mischief on the centreplate handle!) Then the presenter had to get in and sort out how everything works—and just for good measure his dog jumped in too.

".... sailing is really easy to learn......"

Well, I'm a true professional, of course, so I took it all in my stride and we wobbled off across the river. I tried to make it easy on the helmsman who was giving a running commentary to camera whilst keeping the dog from getting tangled in the mainsheet and steering an unfamiliar boat on a busy river in a sluicing tide.

The camera work over, the producer took me for a spin, just for fun, and finally my skipper took me home. Now, she usually makes a mess of picking up the mooring buoy which is in front of the Royal Burnham Yacht Club, at that time of the evening full of expert sailors drinking gin and gazing out of the window. 'Please!' I begged her, 'don't make a mess of it tonight! Remember I'm a star!'

Well, she managed it — not very elegantly done but she picked up the mooring first time. The snag was, she forgot to fetch the dinghy to get ashore with, and that was over on the pontoon, so we had to cast off again and row over to get it. Never mind, what a day!

Picking up a mooring should always be done calmly and in control.....

HURRICANE!

26th and 27th October 2002

It was October and I was still on my mooring, along with the other scows. Now, this is not normally a problem; I'm all for a nice long sailing season and my skipper is ever the optimist. 'We get some lovely mild sailing days in October!' she says to her chums, 'Let's make the most of the year!' Their keenness usually evaporates after September, though, and many lovely sailing days are wasted while they drink coffee in the club bar and mutter things like 'It would be a lovely wind if it wasn't so cold!'.

Anyway, this October weather was giving me a funny feeling in my bilges, and I knew something was brewing. It started to blow on the Saturday night; by Sunday morning I wouldn't be exaggerating to say it was up to a force 10 and you could feel there was worse to come. What a night! I was clinging on to my mooring line for dear life, and have never known the river so rough. It rained in torrents, which was a blessing in a way as the weight of water in my canvas cover stopped it blowing off and taking flight.

Other scows were less fortunate; those without covers were filling up and sinking fast, rudders and gear floating away on the tide. Somehow we all managed to hang on to our moorings, though poor Raffles had obviously decided she'd had enough, and when daylight came we were horrified to see her upside down and impaled on her own mast. I could hardly bear to look.

Dawn gave us a respite, as the tide ebbed and left us exhausted but safe on the mud. It must have been a big tide as we're normally afloat, but it was a blessing as it gave us a chance to rest. Those who had filled up and sunk during the night were able to take a breather and have a grumble about their waterlogged state. I have to say we were all pretty soggy; I was half full of water and feeling distinctly sluggish. I certainly didn't fancy my chances of being able to stay afloat when the tide came in.

Meanwhile the wind was rising still further and all we could do was wait patiently, hoping our owners would see the danger and come to our rescue. To pass the time we watched the bigger boats bouncing on their moorings further out in deeper water, trying to keep our spirits up by laying bets on which of the racing keelboats would sink next. On the moored yachts sails were working loose and being blown to shreds; this wind would keep the sailmakers busy all winter! In the back of our mind, though, we were all anxious. None of us would survive another tide.

By mid morning we were relieved to see that our prayers had been answered when a motley assortment of humans tumbled out of cars and staggered onto the pontoon. They hung about dithering for what seemed like an eternity before realising they had no choice but to get us to safety. One at a time they plunged into the mud which was cold, wet and up to their knees. You should have heard the language! Cursing and squelching, they floundered out to our moorings to assess the damage.

Their first task was to bail us out, which took a long time but what a relief! The next stage was trickier as it involved dragging us one by one through the mud and heaving us onto the pontoon. We were all sodden and extra heavy; the soft mud gave them no grip and it was so hard not to giggle as they pushed, pulled, cursed and occasionally slipped, falling flat on their faces in the mud.

Luckily I was nearest to the pontoon, so I was first out. It seemed to take them forever to move me - that mud is a powerful glue

and I ended up covered in it, but I suppose this was no time to be worrying about my appearance!

Humans may not be that bright but their hearts are in the right place, bless them! More and more people were joining in the rescue which was just as well, as heaving me from mud to pontoon took the combined efforts of about six people. I was safe, but there were six other scows to go! I didn't envy the humans as they leapt back into the mud and repeated the struggle six more times, over increasingly longer distances.

Getting poor old Raffles off her mast gave them a particular headache as the mast had driven itself deep into the mud, but finally it was done. She'll survive, given a bit of emergency surgery from a competent shipwright. We are so resilient!

Now here's a strange thing. It took several hours to rescue all of us, hours that we would not normally have had as the tide had been due back in long before the job was done. But the wind, now up to force 12, had obligingly held back the tide so not only was it lower than I had ever seen it but it stayed out for several hours! If the water had risen before we were all safe, it would have been a watery grave for those left behind.

It took another age to get us onto our trailers, one at a time, and up the slipway to the shelter of the dinghy park. The poor humans, now covered in mud from stem to stern, hesitated on the quayside. It was easy to see the dilemma that faced them – whether to go home and clean themselves up, or whether to head for the bar for some much needed refreshment and risk covering the yacht club carpet in mud!

Well, it was no contest, really. In spite of furious mutterings from a disgruntled bar steward, a trail of muddy footprints revealed that they spent a happy afternoon sharing a few well deserved drinks, no doubt regaling all comers with the tale of their daring six-boat rescue in the teeth of the hurricane. The bar also gave everyone a grandstand view of rest of the moored boats taking their punishment as the tide finally fought its way back in to the river and punched into the wind-driven waves coming the other way. Not a pretty sight.

What a weekend! I've ended up covered in mud, dishevelled but safe – glad to say I've survived a hurricane and lived to sail another day!

Yachting babe.... with a dash of mud

SWALLOWS AND AMAZONS FOR EVER!

Every year a fleet of small boats heads to the Walton Backwaters in Essex to take part in a Swallows and Amazons weekend, racing and cruising on the network of creeks and islands familiar to readers of Arthur Ransome's 'Secret Water'. The event is an open boats rally organised by the Old Gaffers Association. This year a good time was had by all, as Buttercup's own log reveals.....

Saturday 12th July 2003

It's Swallows and Amazons weekend again! I'll gloss over the discomfort of being heaved onto a trailer and towed up the A12 at speeds that make my stringers ache, but it's all worth it to get to Walton Backwaters and sail in company with so many other boats, including a whole fleet of fellow scows (nine of us this year, not all from Burnham! Must get together for a good gossip....)

Scows rounding the mark...

I always get a chance to look my best, dressed overall and flying all my flags. Skipper usually makes a bit of an effort, polishes up the yellow paint on my foredeck and picks all the beer bottle tops out of my floorboards.

As we sailed down Foundry Creek to the start of the round the island race, all the scow skippers were in a panic because as usual they couldn't work out which start gun was which or where the line was. Honestly, they're hopeless! You just can't get the staff. At least they managed to work out which way round the island we were meant to be racing.

Finally we were off, up the Twizzle, more or less at the right time with a lovely south easterly breeze. This was more like it! I got to pass the time with the other boats at the back of the fleet whilst the skippers exchanged comments. It always makes my varnish glow to hear people say 'Is that a West Wight scow? Isn't she lovely!'

If I had a decent skipper I'd have been a lot further up the fleet. All the other scows were well ahead; she had set my jib for some extra speed—all very admirable but the halliard was not tight enough and she was too busy taking photos, chatting to passing boats and eating ham sandwiches to concentrate properly. My talents are wasted!

The wind came astern and the tide against us as we rounded the exposed end of Horsey Island but I don't mind a bit of a chop and usually manage to keep my skipper dry. After a careful gybe we flew up Hamford water with a fine wind astern - brilliant!

The sailing was trickier as we rounded Skipper's Island and the wind came forward. I think there were only a couple of boats astern of us by then (and one was an Optimist so that doesn't really count).

I was now in for a tricky bit of windward work against the tide—not my strong point, I have to confess, so I was pleased to see that my skipper was concentrating at last (she must have finished her sandwiches). We made surprisingly good progress, helped by my being prepared to stick my nose into the grass at the end of each tack.

A couple of nice long tacks across the Red Sea (Horsey Mere to the uneducated) brought us to a fair tide again. We seem to have had a stroke of luck, as we found we'd passed the other scows! That makes a change. We decided to go for it! Fast tacking with the tide past Titchmarsh marina brought us to the head of Foundry Creek where the wind freed us but it was flukey and we were fighting the tide again in a narrow winding channel. Suddenly I could feel the tiller wobble and my skipper's weight shift forward— she was trying to reach the bottle opener! This would not do; the other scows were coming up fast astern and this was not the time for a beer. A quick bounce from me knocked it out of reach; that did it. She focussed on the clubhouse bar and finish line with a glazed look on her face.

A finish gun for first scow home; there's a novelty (for her at least!). What a race!

Sunday 13th July

There was no racing today but a nice easterly breeze, a treasure hunt for those who wanted it and a rendezvous at Stone Point for a picnic lunch. As soon as there was enough water in Foundry Creek we all set off to see if we could sail the other way round Horsey Island. Together with fellow scows Harlequin, Waterwitch, Lowly Worm, Mrs Tiggywinkle and Periwinkle (they do give us daft names, don't they....), we turned left at the top of Foundry Creek and headed down the Twizzle, past Titchmarsh Marina and over the Wade. Crossing Horsey Mere most of the fleet dispersed but the other scows were following me.

By the hesitancy in my tiller I could tell that my skipper was not sure where to go next. I knew she had packed a chart because I heard her say so, but did she have it on board? She did not. 'I can remember the way!' she said confidently, but I'm not so sure - approaching the island from the other direction made everything look very different. Added to which it was still a few hours off high water and it looked as though we were sailing into a damp field.

'It's alright, there's a channel between Horsey and Honey Island' she called out to the others. Hmm, it looked a bit shallow to me but the wind was astern and there was no turning back now.

A startled seal looked up from snoozing on a mud bank and blinked at us as the reeds got thicker and the seagulls were definitely walking not floating. My rudder tickled as it bumped on the mud. Well, if it came to it she'd just have to get out and push, wouldn't she? Her two ten year old crew members were looking a bit apprehensive, as well they might.

There was a shout from behind and it looked as though Harlequin had taken a nose dive into a reed bed. We could see her skipper had climbed out and was knee deep in mud, cursing roundly. Where Buttercup leads, others follow.... if they dare!

One more bump as my rudder bounced on its pintles and then we were through, sailing on water not mud, what a relief. Lowly Worm and Waterwitch were with me but there was no sign of Harlequin and I could feel the hesitancy in my tiller as the skippers debated whether they should go back and look for her. Mine was obviously feeling slightly guilty at having taken the short cut in the first place. We headed back to the start of the shallows, but there was no way of getting any further as it was head to wind and no room to let the centreplate down. A passing boat told us that Harlequin was safely back at the pontoon, given a tow by a rib, and we later found out that her rudder pintle broke when she grounded. No wonder she nose dived into a field!

Meanwhile the rest of us got together again for a beam reach up the west side of Horsey Island. This was perfect sailing - sheltered water, a steady breeze and good company. I bet we all looked gorgeous together, but it's a shame you can't say the same for our skippers. We boats age so much more gracefully than humans, as long as we're looked after; our wood mellows to a rich honey colour that new boats just don't have. Over fifty years old and still attracting admiring glances! I can't say the same for my skipper, and she's a few years younger. Not that I'm conceited or anything.....

So there we were, reaching up Horsey Island with sails trimmed to perfection. Rounding the northwest corner into Hamford Water brought the wind on the nose and the tide was still flooding against us, so I really had to concentrate for this bit. The fleet scattered here, some making long tacks over to the north shore, others like me short tacking close to Horsey to try and cheat the tide.

The two children on board came in handy then - normally they're a bit of a nuisance but useful when it comes to quick work on the jib sheets. They grumbled a bit, wanting to get to their picnic and getting fed up of the tiny bit of progress we were making on each tack. No patience, the younger generation; they have to learn that some things just can't be hurried. I was enjoying the challenge, though, it focuses the mind wonderfully tacking against the tide and it was a smashing breeze.

A couple sitting in the cockpit of an anchored motor boat looked on bemused as it took us at least six tacks to get past them, but eventually we pulled ahead. Engines? Huh!

"Do you think they do it for fun?"

Sods law of tides came into play as we reached the junction of Hamford Water and Walton Creek exactly on high water, so the flood tide we were fighting turned into a fast running ebb against us as we rounded the corner to get across to Stone Point. That's the drawback with sailing round tidal islands! The wind seemed to have turned the corner too, as headwinds are prone to do. We could see the rest of the Swallows and Amazons fleet pulled up on the sandy beach, but it took a few more tacks before we were able to join them. Skipper and crew gratefully tumbled ashore for a hasty beer and sandwich, but all too soon it was time to go again as we had to get back up Foundry Creek and onto the slipway before the tide dropped too far.

Some boats took a tow home so their skippers could finish their beer at leisure, but a few set off under sail. My skipper had a gleam in her eye; she had offloaded the crew and we were going to go for it. It was a challenging sail back as the wind was gusting over the dunes, fine on the port bow, and there was a sluicing ebb but, hey, we're a good team and we had a great time, luffing to each gust and making it home without a tack.

Back at the yacht club there's always a mad scramble with trailers to get boats out in quick succession, the crews struggling to manoeuvre trailers on the muddy slipway before the tide drops too far. It's a shame the day's sailing has to end so soon; the Backwaters are a delight to sail in, but the tides are hellish. Never mind, you can't have everything and now it's back to reality, heaved onto my trailer, ratchet straps so tight they make my frames ache and it's back to the Crouch we go. It was worth it!

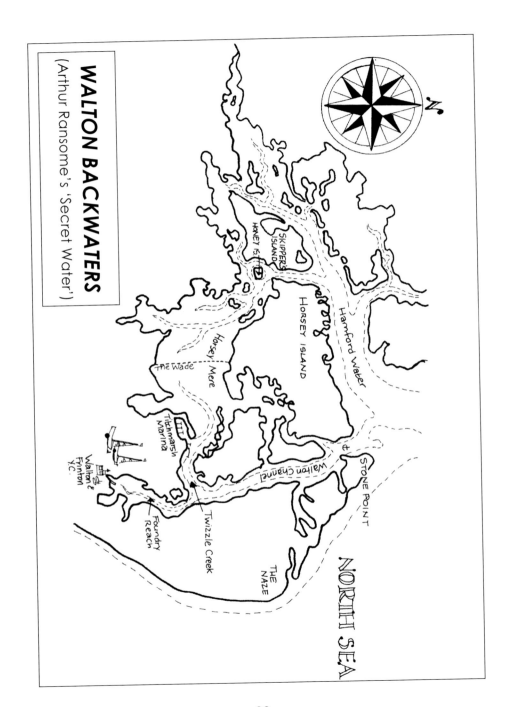

WALTON BACKWATERS
(Arthur Ransome's 'Secret Water')

NORTH SEA

THE SMALLEST CRUISER IN THE CLUB

Saturday 13th September 2003

The yacht club cruisers headed off to West Wick this weekend - which is all of four miles up the Crouch. An adventurous lot, aren't they? We decided to go too; after all, why should the big boats have all the fun? I know I can't compete in the comfy cabin department, but my skipper had made arrangements to bunk down on something more opulent. Suit yourself, I said.

We were late leaving; skipper had to go to London in the morning (what a waste of a good wind!) so I was tugging on my mooring in impatience as the fair tide went by, taking with it the other cruisers on their way up river. It was two o'clock by the time she hurtled down the pontoon and dived on board but, give her credit, she had my sails up and mooring cast off within minutes. I didn't have to remind her that we only had an hour or so of tide left and a long way to go.

Luckily it was a fair wind, an easterly 3, so we shot off like a rocket while she disentangled herself from the mainsheet and tried to find a course that was not on the verge of a gybe. By the time we passed Creeksea she had got herself together and we settled down to enjoy a fabulous sail. A small catamaran - one of those whizzy things - came up fast astern, with her skipper kitted out in wet suit and all the gear.

'Lovely day!' he called out as he hurtled past. 'Lovely', replied my skipper. The catamaran was soon a speck on the horizon. Funny that; he must have had an extra bit of wind that passed us by.

Funny... there must be more wind over there...

In the end our timing was perfect, through the moorings at Fambridge and then right at Stow post for a beam reach up to the marina at just about slack water. Turning into West Wick brought the wind ahead, but we could see our cruising friends urging us on and into a spare berth alongside them. I felt quite proud to be the smallest member of the cruising fleet and eager to explore further up the creek which twists and turns tantalisingly out of sight between mudbanks.

Later, skipper and son took the hint and we went for a potter up the silent creek, mudbanks rising out of a fast ebbing tide. We sailed until we ran aground, pushing off with an oar and startling a heron. Exciting stuff, this long distance cruising! Later still, skipper abandoned me for the lush comforts of a motor cruiser's cabin and I could hear the sound of merriment and clink of glasses. My skipper is so two faced - contemptuous of motor yachts when their wake leaves us lurching out of control, but not too proud to take their hospitality when it's offered, you'll notice.

Sunday 14th September 2003

The next day dawned sunny and warm again with an easterly breeze. Crews were relaxed as none of them could leave until the tide let them later in the day. They spent the morning breakfasting ashore, walking and even fruit picking, all totally pointless (I was going to say fruitless) activities as far as I'm concerned. As the tide trickled in I was itching to explore the other side of Stow Creek but had to wait while skipper and her family filled up bags of sloes and wild plums and drank endless cups of coffee in their friends' cabins.

Eventually she relented and jumped in, along with Whispaire's skipper who had foolishly left her scow at home. A grazing cow looked up in surprise as we sailed and bumped our way into the heart of the Essex countryside. Getting out of those tiny gullies and creeks proved rather challenging as the tide was by then pouring into them, but after judicious use of oars and curses we made it back to the marina. Not so much mucking around in boats as boating around in the muck!

No, it's your turn to get out and push.....

When it came to departure time my skipper, for whom caution is always the better part of valour (and anyway she hates getting wet) decided to let Whispaire tow me home without her. She claimed it was because we wouldn't be able to beat home against the tide and a freshening easterly wind, but I think secretly she has been seduced by good living and wanted to act out some sad fantasy by posing on the deck of a motor yacht. What a two faced tart!

She did get wet in the end though, you'll be pleased to hear, later in the day when she picked me up from Whispaire's berth in the marina to take me back to my mooring. This should have been a short and easy sail but the wind had freshened and kicked up a nasty sea against the ebbing tide so she had a horrible lumpy beat after all. She ended up soaking wet and scared witless - serves her right for fawning over motor yachts!

BUTTERCUP CLIMBS A MOUNTAIN

After moving to West Wales Buttercup found new sailing opportunities in places that were as different as could be from her east coast and Solent waters. One weekend her skipper accepted an invitation to join in a small boat rally in mid Wales – a challenging experience for both boat and skipper!

Saturday 14th May 2005

She has got to be joking - no way am I going sailing on *that*! After driving for miles up winding mountain roads (mountains? I'm a boat not a goat!) we paused at the top of a hill to open a gate; the road dipped down alarmingly towards an expanse of slate black water, whipped into white crests by a strong easterly wind. Where on earth has she brought me?

Unbelievably, at the bottom of the hill was a tiny sailing club, with a row of dinghies and a slipway. I couldn't help noticing that most of the dinghies had floats attached to the mast to help right them when they capsize. My skipper pulled up alongside a few fellow wooden boats on trailers, and joined their owners who were standing around looking at the weather and commenting occasionally 'It does seem to be easing up a bit'. 'Easing up', my forefoot! It was blowing a six gusting seven straight down the sides of the hills and waves were breaking onto the slipway. There would be no sailing today.

My skipper may be incompetent but fortunately she is terrified of strong winds, so I settled down for a quiet afternoon on my trailer chatting to the others. There was a nice looking Scottish double ender and a few other wooden boats; I'm not a snob or anything, you understand, but anyone with varnish that gleams as much as mine is usually worth getting to know. Madam disappeared off with her chums to try and put her tent up, no easy feat in this wind; she seemed to be sitting on it to stop it blowing away while her friends worked out how to put it up.

It blew hard for the rest of the day; I could have told them it would. By the time they staggered out of the clubhouse at midnight, singing sea shanties out of tune, the wind had died completely. 'Let's go sailing!' one of them shouted. Ha ha, very funny.

Sunday 15th May

By dawn the lake was transformed. The dark grey menacing water was now a soft blue reflecting a cloudless sky; the gentlest of breezes beckoned. And where was my skipper? Snoring in her tent, that's where! Her friend Mike who organised the rally is a jolly sensible chap; by 6.30am he had pushed 'Aquarius' down the slip and sailed away across the lake. I was itching to join them! Luckily, she staggered out of her tent at 7.30 looking a bit bleary eyed, but caught the mood of the day and rigged me with almost indecent haste; I was down the slip and into the water before you can say 'damn, I forgot the burgee'. Gordon had launched his little boat and set off too, so there were two red sails and one cream adding to the colour of the day.

Now, this is my first sail of the season, and I've been sitting on a trailer in all weathers for six months, so I think it's a bit unkind of my skipper to call me a leaky old tub. What does she expect! She used to make sure I lay in lots of lovely East coast mud at low tide so I could wriggle it into all my gaps, and I don't think much of this fresh water; at my age I need plenty of salt mud packs to keep me going. I told her to get bailing and stop complaining. It's all very well sailing in new places, but she should have a bit more consideration for my needs.

Anyway, enough grumbling, it's a beautiful day, one in a million and worth waiting for. The wind is too light really for me to perform at my best, but after being blown at by a cold mean easterly all day yesterday, we're happy as long as there's enough to move us. It is the first sail of the year after all, and skipper is usually all fingers and thumbs at the beginning of the season, gets the main sheet in a tangle, drops the halliard too quickly so the gaff drops on her head, you know the kind of thing – so embarrassing! Anyway, this time she seems to have got her act together. The breeze is a bit fickle, bent by the hills into all kinds of directions, but that's her problem, not mine!

Later in the day all the wooden boats set off together through the narrows into the next inlet. It's a strange place – being a reservoir the hills plunged straight down to the water so we could get quite close before tacking. I had quite a shock the first time we approached the shore; it was all very green and pretty, speckled with bluebells and funny white blobs which started moving around and making noises at us. I've never seen anything like it! I'm used to getting quite close to seals, but there's something almost indecent about getting this close to a flock of sheep! At least seals don't baa at you. Whatever next?

Funny looking seals.....

All too soon it was late afternoon as we tacked slowly back in the last of the breeze, enjoying the rich colours of the hills and the light on the water.

I'm back in the front garden now wondering where on earth she'll take me next, and feeling quite proud of the fact that I'm now a high altitude scow!

Clywedog Sailing Club

NEWTOWN
LLANIDLOES

WALES

BURNHAM TALES

If Buttercup has finally finished complaining about her skipper's shortcomings, I might get a word in myself. Much of my sailing with Buttercup and an assortment of bigger boats was on the River Crouch in Essex. Now the greatest problem – and the greatest asset – of the East Coast is mud. If an east coast yachtsman claims never to have gone aground, he's probably either lying or sails a dinghy (on second thoughts, I've got Buttercup stuck in the mud once or twice!).

"I spy with my little eye something beginning with S....."

On the other hand, it's great for anchoring – superglue with attitude. This leads to some very sociable raft ups; the Crouch may be short on beaches but it's long on hospitality. In the best and muddiest anchorages there is unlikely to be anywhere to get ashore, so socialising tends to be done afloat. This is all very well if sociability is what you're after, but there are times when a little privacy up a quiet creek might be just what you intended.....

"Cooee!"

However, it is most people's experience that trying to mix romance and sailing is asking for trouble. Strained relations between skipper and mate are a cause of constant inspiration for cartoons, even in these enlightened times when the wife is as likely to be skipper as mate.

"I'm not pulling any more of your silly ropes unless you say sorry...."

Many cartoons have also arisen out of the sailors' obsession with racing. Now this is something I could never quite get the hang of; all that effort, concentration and heaving on ropes just to end up at the same harbour you started in! I have been known to say 'after you' to someone when rounding a mark to avoid risking Buttercup's varnish by close encounters with other boats. Unsurprisingly, I don't get invited to crew on racing boats very often.....

"I don't think she's quite got that killer instinct...."

During Burnham week, the Crouch is especially full of boats sailing fast in circles. At such times cruisers need to keep well out of the way – if there's room!

"More quiche, Rodney?"

If there's one thing more terrifying than a river full of racers, it's a river full of children. Buttercup and I spent many a Friday evening with a boat load of under 8's who were more interested in making up songs about crocodiles in the Crouch than they were learning which way to move the tiller. Sailing with children brought out the Joyce Grenfell in me, as this piece of blatant plagiarism, performed at a sailing club Christmas party, shows:

THE JUNIOR REGATTA

(with apologies to Joyce Grenfell)

"Good morning children and welcome to our junior regatta. Are your Oppies all rigged and ready to launch? Jolly good! What's the matter, Samantha? Virginia has pinched your mainsheet to try and strangle Oliver? Well, that's not very nice, is it, Virginia! Give Samantha back her mainsheet and will someone please ask Oliver's mummy if he's usually that funny shade of blue.

David, please take that wind indicator out of your ear and put it back on your mast, there's a good boy. What's that? You're an alien from the planet Zog and it's your aerial, is it? Lovely, but can you stop being an alien now put it back on your mast? Thank you, David. (Such an imaginative child! I'm sure he's destined for great things.)

Now, children, we're going to start the day with a little race, so let's all see how fast we can make our little boats go, shall we? What's that, Isabel? Daddy said he'll buy you a Laser if you win? Well that's very nice of your daddy, but we all know that winning isn't everything, don't we, children. We're here to learn and have lots of fun. No George, there won't be a protest committee, and yes, we are using the up to date racing rules.

Now, get your boats up to the start line and I'll be there to tell you what to do.

Can you all hear me, children? I want you to sail over to that orange buoy, round to that one over there and back to me, three times, is that clear? Think carefully about where the wind is coming from, all of you, and what the tide's doing...... what's the matter, Thomas? Well, you should have gone before we left the clubhouse! Do pull the tiller towards you Samantha! Harriet dear, you're going in the wrong direction..... no dear, you can't go home, not yet, just do this little race first!

Two minutes to start...... do put your gameboy away, Freddie and concentrate! Samantha, pull the tiller towards you dear! No, George, you can't call starboard on Oliver. Because you're on the port tack, George, that's why! James, do balance your boat, there's a good chap..... James, do wake up, dear.

(Hoot for start of race) Off you go, everyone! No, Thomas, the other way, that's right, just follow the others...... Samantha, push the tiller away from you! Now, Samantha! Oh dear. Just swim round to the other side of the boat, stand on the dagger board and pull yourself up again, there's a good girl. Harriet, do come away from those moored boats.

Harriet, steer away from that moored yacht. Push the tiller away from you, Harriet. No, I said push! Oh dear, too late!

George... don't do that! Because it's against the rules to ram the boat in front of you, that's why! Careful when you gybe Samantha.... Pull the tiller towards you.... no, towards you... oh dear.

Now, swim round to the other side of the boat and get onto the dagger board to pull yourself up.... Well done, Samantha.

Has anyone been counting laps? Charlotte, do bail your boat, you're sitting in a puddle... no, don't chuck the water all over Samantha.... I said DON'T, Charlotte... well, because it's not very nice, that's why! Samantha, do stop crying! You're wet already!

Lucy, sail over here, dear, you're heading for the mud.... oh dear.... pull your dagger board up and gybe round, there's a good girl. No, Lucy, don't get out of your boat and push! I said don't get out and...... oh. Such a soft patch of mud, that one. Now don't cry, Lucy, Mummy won't mind getting you all cleaned up when you come ashore, of course she won't!

Now, last time round, children, centreboards up and let those mainsheets out...... no, tiller towards you, Samantha! Oh dear, never mind. Swim round to the other side of the boat..... yes, that's

right.... I say, Samantha, those aren't very nice words for a little girl to be using! No, even if she is wet and fed up and her boat is upside down.

Thomas, you're supposed to go round the buoy, not straight over the top of it! Now, everyone, head straight for the finish. Is someone writing down positions?

Is everyone back on shore? Good. I want to say well done, everybody, you all sailed brilliantly. Yes, even you, Samantha. No, don't sulk, Isabel, there's nothing wrong with coming last, nothing at all.... Who is making that squeaky noise? Well, stop it Oliver! You'll ruin your life jacket! Now, before lunch I think we should have a little talk about sail trim..... stop, where are you all going? Oh, lunch is ready is it? We'll have our little chat after lunch shall we?

So rewarding, working with children, isn't it? Amazing to think that these children might be our future Olympic champions...... Neville! Stop picking your nose or you'll never be a famous sailor when you grow up! "

NOTHING LIKE THE FIRST TIME

Unlike the little darlings on the previous pages, my sailing career didn't start in a dinghy at the age of six. I first set foot on a boat when a group of us in our early twenties chartered a 33 foot yacht and went cruising in the West Country for a week. We knew almost nothing about sailing, even our skipper, who was chosen for the task by virtue of being a Cornishman and thus having seafaring coursing through his veins—somewhere.

Our first mate was elected on the basis that he had read a great many books on the subject and always carried a small length of rope in his pocket to practise knot tying. Then there was the second mate (who had done a bit of dinghy sailing) and the Purser, who was in charge of supplies as well as being Medical Officer. Running rapidly out of titles the rest of us were nominated Able Seaman (if we knew how to tie on a fender) or Midshipman (if we didn't).

This determination to do things properly and give everyone a title betrayed the fact that our nautical know-how came by and large from 'Swallows and Amazons', Hornblower books, fragments of naval history and a vague belief in the seafaring greatness of the British Nation. This was a heady brew, bestowing an optimism and confidence in our abilities that far outstripped the reality.

Our first week afloat was in March when charter fees were cheap; by degrees we found out why. To make our holiday cheaper still we had taken the brochure literally when it described our chosen vessel as having seven berths. I will never forget the day when, crammed into two cars with all our luggage and provisions for a week (including a large bag of oranges to prevent scurvy), we arrived in Falmouth in a fever of anticipation. As we unloaded onto the pontoon, gazing in awe upon our very own ship, our skipper tried to conceal the extent of his ignorance from the owner who was showing him the ropes. Nodding vigorously he could be heard to mumble things like 'Ah yes, the topping lift'. No wonder we were given a cruising range that could have been sailed on the end of a long piece of string.

I had spent several weeks wondering what a 33 foot yacht looked like. As we climbed aboard and faced the gleaming fibreglass and fitted carpets, I was suitably impressed, though it took some time to find the seven berths, some of which required great agility and no luggage.

We had yet to discover how sleeping three in a foc'sle can strain friendships, and how breakfast has to wait until until those sleeping on the bunk that converts to the table have woken up and put their sleeping bags away. But ignorance is bliss; we did not know that crowding seven onto a small yacht in March is not generally considered enjoyable, so accordingly we had the time of our lives. We took pleasure in saying 'aye aye skipper', and savouring phrases like 'ready about' and 'abaft the beam'. The boat may have been modern but the spirit was pure Arthur Ransome.

During that first cruise the rain lashed down, the gales blew, our hired oilskins leaked and we were flattened by sea sickness. Yet we still came back in September desperate for more.

Looking back, it sounds irresponsible to do what we did, but in spite of having no experience (or perhaps because of it), we took our responsibilities seriously and nothing for granted. Before setting off skipper gave us a safety briefing and no line was cast off until we were all in harnesses and clipped on. Short coastal passages were planned with the thoroughness of an ocean voyage and log painstakingly filled in every hour. Given that electronic navigation was at this time still only a twinkle in an engineer's eye, we knew there would be no second chances; we read all the sailing manuals we could get our hands on and practised endless man overboard drill with a fender, just for the fun of it.

One problem with chartering is that there is always a deadline; the yacht has to be back in her home port on a certain day or someone else's holiday gets ruined. This meant that on one occasion we were the only boat weighing anchor in St Mary's Sound in the Scillies with a southwesterly force 7 blowing and worse to come. Our first gale!

We left on the evening tide after extensive preparations; from seasickness pills to safe stowage, sandwiches and safety harnesses, storm jib and sobering extracts from Heavy Weather Sailing read out loud, we were as mentally and physically prepared as a seasoned Cape Horner for our dash back to Falmouth.

It was a wild and awe inspiring passage, my first experience of a moonlit sea heaped into silver hills by a following gale. Most of us were seasick beyond our wildest nightmares but our Cornish skipper's seafaring sense did us proud and we sailed wetly, proudly and on time into Falmouth, enjoying the euphoria that comes with not feeling sick any more.

Since those days I learned the delights of sailing in summer weather, in my own boat, wearing my own oilskins. I went to navigation classes, learnt how to cope with seasickness and make tea in the sink to avoid scalds. But somehow the memory of those first few years remains fresh—uncomfortable and inept it may have been but there is nothing quite like the first time!

AND FINALLY......

A song dedicated to river sailors everywhere:

WHEN THE WIND IS FROM THE EAST

(tune: 'A policeman's lot is not a happy one')

When the wind is from the east it goes right through you
(goes right through you)
And when it's from the west it pours with rain (pours with rain)
And when you've tacked the whole way down the river
(down the river)
It will turn and make you tack back home again (home again)
And half the time you're sitting on a mudbank (on a mudbank)
Pretending that you stopped there just for lunch (just for lunch)
Ah, take one consideration with another (with another)
We sailors are a masochistic bunch, oooooh.....

We like sitting on a mudbank just for lunch (just for lunch)
We sailors are a masochistic bunch ('chistic bunch)

And every now and then we go out racing (go out racing)
So even when we're last again we've tried ('gain we've tried)
And we're out in half a gale with lee rail under (lee rail under)
Or becalmed and drifting backwards on the tide (on the tide)
And half the time you wish the race was over (race was over)
And you'd be safely tucked up in the bar (in the bar)
Ah, take one consideration with another (with another)
We sailors rarely sail very far, oooooh.....

We'd rather be a-drinking in the bar (in the bar)
For we sailors rarely sail very far (very far)